HOW TO HANDLE CRANKY CUSTOMER PROBLEMS USING BEHAVIORAL SCIENCE

A Humanist Learning Systems Companion Book

By Jennifer Hancock

Published by Jennifer Hancock
Copyright 2018 by Jennifer Hancock
Published 2018
ISBN: 9781731105363
Imprint: Independently published

Title: How to Handle Cranky Customer Problems Using Behavioral Science

Paperback Edition

Author: Jennifer Hancock
　　　Editor: Desiree Vogelpohl
Publisher: Humanist Learning Systems.

This book is also available as an ebook and audio book at most online retailers

All rights reserved. No part of this book may be used or reproduced in any manner whatsoever without written permission, except in the case of brief quotations embodied in critical articles or reviews.

TABLE OF CONTENTS

Table of Contents 3

Chapter 1: Introduction 5

   Overview 5

   Topics Discussed in this Book 6

Chapter 2: Why Are People So Cranky? 7

Chapter 3: Don't Get Pulled into the Drama .. 11

   Understanding that their behavior is not about you does two things for you 12

Chapter 4: Understanding Your Response 15

   The Science of Response 15

   For Instance: 17

   Helping Clients Calm Down 19

Chapter 5: An Example 21

Chapter 6: Don't Fake It 23

Chapter 7: About the Author 25

~~~~~

4

CHAPTER 1: INTRODUCTION

I teach how to stop abusive and bullying behavior using behavioral science techniques called operant conditioning. I learned these techniques in college where I worked for a dolphin language cognition lab. These conditioning techniques do work on humans and understanding how people are conditioned to respond, and how you too are conditioned to respond, helps you to not be conditioned by the conditions you find yourself in. To put that in English – knowing how and why you respond the way you do helps you to NOT respond negatively when negativity is thrown at you.

An amazing thing happens when you can control your response, which is that the person who best controls their response, controls the dynamic! This is a skill worth learning. It applies to pretty much everything in your life. All interpersonal dynamics are driven by this. Seriously, get my book, *The Bully Vaccine,* or take one of my online classes where I teach this in depth.

This book is a short overview of how this concept applies to handling cranky customers.

Overview

Without customers, we don't have a business. But what can, or should we do if one of our customers is cranky?

Answer: Learn why people behave how they do and how you can respond so that you can be happier and more effectively help solve your customer's problems without getting pulled into their drama, whatever that is.

This book discusses how your responses impact your customer so that you can choose a response that will help you stand your ground while still being compassionate about your customer's problem. The goal here is to help you learn how to respond professionally even in situations where the people around you are freaking out.

This is the companion book to the online course *How to Handle Cranky Customer Problems Using Behavioral Science*. It contains transcripts of the course for easy home reference. Individuals and groups can benefit from this course. For more information, visit: https://humanistlearning.com/crankycustomers/

Topics Discussed in this Book

We are going to talk about why people behave the way that they do and how you can use that knowledge to control how you respond. And, how controlling how you respond will help you be happier and help you solve your customer's problems, all without getting pulled into their drama.

~~~~~

CHAPTER 2: WHY ARE PEOPLE SO CRANKY?

Let's start with the first obvious questions: Why are people so cranky? Why are they so negative? Are they like this with everyone?

We humans are creatures of habit. We are conditioned to respond to certain things in certain ways. People who are cranky are almost always actually scared. The great sage Yoda once said, "Fear leads to anger, anger leads to hate, and hate leads to suffering." People who are cranky are usually trying to defend themselves from perceived or imagined threats and this is how they have learned how to cope.

Is it a good way to cope? No, they are suffering for it. The problem is that if they are your customer, then all their fears, insecurities, and negativity are being directed at you!

We all have our triggers. No one gets through life unscathed. These triggers are conditioned responses. When something happens, we respond and those responses have been learned and reinforced over our entire lives. For instance, if every time a whistle is blown and something bad happens, you will learn to be afraid when a whistle is blown. That is what conditioning is. We are all impacted by this.

Every interaction we have is a learning experience. Sometimes good things happen (positive reinforcement). Sometimes bad things happen (negative reinforcement). And sometimes nothing happens, a neutral response (non-reinforcement). The combination of positive, negative, and neutral reinforcements shape our behaviors over time. Most of us aren't even aware that it's happening, but it is.

What happens when you start paying attention to people's responses and your own response to their response? You break the cycle! It becomes a lot easier to understand why someone, in certain situations, acts horribly or crankily. Previous experience has taught them to behave this way. They may anticipate negative experiences. Their negative behavior causes a negative experience and they end up in a self-reinforcing loop of negative expectation with negative experience. It's actually pretty sad when you think about it. People who are cranky are cranky because they learned to be cranky.

The truth is, you have NO idea what this person has been through. You don't know if they recently lost a child or a spouse, or if they were just laid off. You don't know whether they are cranky strategically or because of overwhelming sadness and fear. And if it's fear, you don't know what caused them to have that much fear.

My point is that their crankiness towards you probably isn't about you at all. They may be diabetic and their blood sugar is low and it is affecting their thinking. They may not feel well and it is all they can do to even be out of bed. Whatever is making them cranky is about them and their life experiences that brought them to this point. You have your own problems.

~~~~~

CHAPTER 3: DON'T GET PULLED INTO THE DRAMA

Like your cranky customer, you also have been conditioned throughout the course of your life. You have your own set of triggers and weird behaviors that you don't control well. You have your own limitations in terms of mental health functioning, physical health issues that affect your mental health, and an entire lifetime of facing a world that isn't always nice to you. We all have scars and we are all sensitive. Some of us more than others. Combine someone who is suffering, and spreading their suffering around through general crankiness, and add them to your suffering. It's not a good combination.

How do you create boundaries and not get pulled into their drama and not allow their crankiness to trigger your crankiness? And can you do this while still assisting them?

First, understand their behavior isn't about you even if it is directed at you! They are cranky with us and we don't want them to be because it makes us feel bad or it triggers our insecurities in some way. You have no idea why this person is behaving this way and that's ok. You don't need to. You just have to accept that they are behaving badly. We cause ourselves an amazing amount of frustration by trying to make other people behave better. It's a futile thing to do because you can't change other people's behavior. Heck, most of us can't even change our own!

Understanding that their behavior is not about you does two things for you

You stop making it about you and you stop trying to make them change.

If someone is cranky because there is a whole lot that has happened in their lives, then it is silly to get mad at them for not being perfectly wonderful to you. That is about you and as long as you are focused on how they are impacting you, you will be stuck in a fruitless loop of insecurity. Your insecurity feeding off of theirs and around and around you go.

If you accept that this is just who they are and you don't know why they are behaving this way but that they probably have a good reason to be this way, then you won't get sucked into the drama! You stop trying to make them be better for your sake, and get on with dealing with them as they are, as best you can.

The key to making this work is humility and compassion. Humility to know your own emotional limitations and stressors and compassion to understand that others may be suffering and stressing too. Whatever is causing this person to behave the way that they are, they have their own stuff going on and they are responding to it as best they can. Treat them with compassion.

~~~~~

CHAPTER 4: UNDERSTANDING YOUR RESPONSE

Let's focus on understanding your response.

Interpersonal interactions are like a dance. Person 1 does something and person 2 responds. Person 1 responds to what person 2 does and they trade responses back and forth. It's an interaction. In the case of a cranky customer, they are being cranky and you are responding to their crankiness, and they are responding to how you responded to them.

Understanding that your response will have an impact on how the other person responds is the key to interpersonal enlightenment. You, despite all your triggers, have the ability to choose how you respond! That's great news. The problem is, what sort of response is going to help a cranky person be less cranky? The answer is, in general, a neutral and polite response will. Let's dive into the science first and then talk about how we use this information in reality.

The Science of Response

There are three types of responses:

- Positive – where you do something the other person likes.

- Negative – where you do something the other person doesn't like.

- Neutral – where what you did wasn't good or bad for the other person. It's just – neutral.

When we deal with people who are difficult, we tend to respond negatively. That is to be expected. We may get cranky back at them. We may decide we don't want to deal with them and get passive aggressive. We may try to pretend to be nice while thinking negative, horrid thoughts, and then are surprised when the person picks up on that, despite us pretending to be nice.

What you need to understand is that from a behavioral conditioning perspective – negative reinforcement is still reinforcement. It actually makes the cranky behavior worse! This is pretty obvious. Fighting cranky stupidity with cranky stupidity is pretty stupid. All that the cranky person learns from you being cranky back at them is that their crankiness was totally justified.

What is counter intuitive is that being nice doesn't work either. We have all had the experience where someone is nasty to us, and we respond by being genuinely nice, and they lash out at us. There is a reason for that which is that positive reinforcement is also reinforcement.

Here is the basic problem. When you are nice, what you are teaching the cranky person is that if I am cranky, people are nice to me. That means that they will do it more because being cranky worked!

The best response to a cranky person is an emotionally neutral response. In order to get people to stop behaving badly, you have to stop rewarding them for behaving badly. I'm not saying don't be nice to them. I'm saying be nice to them when they are nice to you, but don't be mean to them either!

What you want to do is not reward the crankiness while still engaging with the person positively. What you should do is not respond to the cranky but instead redirect towards a positive interaction, which you can then positively respond to.

For Instance:

Say you have a frazzled customer who is frantic and blaming you for the fact that you can't turn around their request in the time they want or for the price they want. And their crankiness at you is misplaced because it's their fault for not coming to you sooner or giving themselves enough lead time to get the project done right. They are yelling at you! What do you do? Well, you could yell back but that would be a negative response and a great way to lose a customer.

You could apologize and do your best. That would be the positive response. But all you will have taught them is that being cranky with you is the best way to bully you into doing work you either shouldn't be doing, or at a price you shouldn't, or at a level of quality that isn't up to your standards. That's not good either.

Your third option is to remain calm which is the neutral response. Sympathize with their plight. Understand that when they yell at you, they are doing so because they can't really yell at themselves. Don't get baited into their drama. This is their problem, not yours, and if they want you to help them, they have to be calm and allow you to help them.

Notice the focus here. You are willing to help – if they will let you help them! As long as they are being cranky, they aren't allowing you to help them. To pull this off, don't get frazzled. Stand your ground politely and calmly with as little emotion as you can muster and say something along the lines of:

"I'm sorry Dave, but I can't do that. I understand you are under a deadline (or whatever else the problem is), but what you want can't be done because (whatever the reason is). I'm sorry, but perhaps we can solve your problem another way?"

Notice that this is calm, sympathetic, and helpful. But you didn't solve their problem for them. What you did is ask them calmly IF they want you to help solve their current problem. It doesn't really matter what you say as long as it is factual and is said calmly and opens the door to problem solving. If they don't want you to solve their problem because all they want to do is rant – great! Don't waste your time trying to solve their problem. Until they are ready to solve the problem, there is nothing you can do but listen.

If that's where they are, just keep repeating your calm – "I understand, but … do you want me to help you?" statement. Only try to solve their problem if they ask you to. If they do, then suggest alternatives that will work such as compromises. "Perhaps if we didn't do this but did this – you could still get this out on time." As long as they are emotionally agitated, you stay calm. If they are frantic then slow down – deliberately. Counter their cranky franticness with calm deliberateness. You are modeling the emotional state you want them to get to.

Helping Clients Calm Down

Yes, this is a lot like helping a kid with a tantrum. In fact, it's everything like helping a kid cope with a tantrum. You remain calm and encourage them to be calm as well. If they can't calm down, that's fine. Sympathize with their anxiety and let them know that you will help them however you can, when they are ready to discuss realistic alternatives.

The point is to remain calm and don't be bullied into doing something you know is wrong. If you lose the deal to someone who gave in to the bullying, that's fine. You don't need that sort of client anyway. If they come back, they will probably turn into one of your best clients. In my experience, the people who were the crankiest turn into my greatest supporters because I helped them overcome their cranky to get to a solution that actually worked for them.

~~~~~

CHAPTER 5: AN EXAMPLE

Let me give you a real-life example of a customer service rep dealing with a cranky customer. I had to rent a car once. I had gone to the rental office and in front of me was a guy who was cranky. I mean REALLY cranky. He needed to re-rent a car he had for a month already. He had to fill out new paperwork and he was REALLY cranky about it. He didn't understand why it needed to be done. All his information was in the computer, why does he have to sign the form again etc etc etc.

The clerk didn't argue with the guy. He just said, "I understand, but I need you to sign this form to extend the rental past one month." He let the guy rant and rave and complain loudly, and he just did the paperwork. He didn't get mad or flustered or upset. He just didn't respond. He did the work that needed to be done as professionally as he could and that was it. He did his job.

It was a perfect response because the customer wasn't actually mad at the clerk. He was mad at the dealership who hadn't fixed his car after a month of working on it which is why he was forced to have a rental car. This guy's anger wasn't even directed at the right person.

The staff could have gotten flustered. But what good would that have done?

- Would it have helped the customer? No.
- Would it have helped the staff feel better? No.
- Would it have helped the other customers who were witnessing this man's performance? No.

Remaining calm and allowing this guy to vent while calmly solving his problem, despite his crankiness at having the problem at all, was the best response. After the cranky guy left, I complimented the staff on doing an amazing job in the face of such negativity. They just shrugged. They did what they needed to do to help the guy solve his problem even if he wasn't appreciative. They didn't let the cranky guy get to them. They didn't fight or get pulled into his drama. They didn't insist he not be cranky. They just remained calm and did their job as best they could. That's how you deal with cranky customers.

Did the cranky customer get what he wanted, which was to not sign the paperwork? No. But, he still left with what he needed, which was an extended rental car contract. As much as this man wanted to fight with the staff, they didn't fight him, and they didn't give in to his demands. Yet, they still helped him professionally and compassionately.

~~~~~

CHAPTER 6: DON'T FAKE IT

There is one last thing I want to caution you on which is that remaining calm is a skill that has to be practiced. Being calm is not something you can fake. Most humans are really adept at reading body language and tone of voice. We understand the meaning and the emotional intent even if it isn't said out loud.

You can't remain calm and emotionally neutral if you are thinking nasty horrible things about the cranky people you encounter. They will hear your nastiness come out. Seriously, they will. This is why you need to feel compassion for them. Remember at the beginning I talked about why people are cranky? I did that so that instead of you being cranky that the other person is cranky, you will feel compassion for them instead. Your compassion will help you respond to the person more authentically so that what you want them to hear is what they actually hear, which is you being calm and compassionate despite their crankiness.

Feeling sorry for them will ensure that your communication with them isn't laced with malice, but with compassion and helpfulness instead. And again, this isn't something you can fake. If you just can't respect someone, pity them instead and try to think of them compassionately. What you may just find is that when you stop treating them as if they are a threat to you or that you hate them, they will stop responding to you as if you are a threat to them! Communication is a two-way street. If you hate someone, they will respond to that hate even if you don't say it out loud. The best way to ensure your communication is as polite and respectful as you would like it to be is to feel compassion, even for the people who are unbelievably cranky.

~~~~~

CHAPTER 7: ABOUT THE AUTHOR

Jennifer Hancock is a mom, author of several books, and founder of Humanist Learning Systems. Jennifer is unique in that she was raised as a freethinker and is considered one of the top speakers and writers in the world of Humanism today. Her professional background is varied including stints in both the for-profit and nonprofit sectors. She has served as Director of Volunteer Services for the Los Angeles SPCA, sold international franchise licenses for a biotech firm, was the Manager of Acquisition Group Information for a half-billion-dollar company, and served as the executive director for the Humanists of Florida. When she became a mother, she decided to stay at home, but that didn't last long. Shortly after her son was born, she published her first book, *The Humanist Approach to Happiness: Practical Wisdom.* Her speaking and teaching business coalesced into the founding of Humanist Learning Systems which provides online personal and professional development training in humanistic business management and science-based harassment training that actually works.

More Learning from Jennifer Hancock

OTHER BOOKS BY JENNIFER HANCOCK
- The Humanist Approach to Happiness
- Jen Hancock's Handy Humanism Handbook
- The Bully Vaccine
- The Humanist Approach to Grief and Grieving
- How to Win Arguments Without Arguing
- Ending Harassment & Retaliation in the Workplace
- Why Bullies Bully & How to Stop Them Using Science
- Reality Based Decision Making for Effective Strategy Development

COURSES TAUGHT BY JENNIFER HANCOCK
- Workplace Bullying for HR professionals
- Living Made Simpler
- An Introduction to Humanism
- Socratic Jujitsu: How to Win Arguments Without Argument
- Why Conflict Resolution Doesn't Work When the Problem is Bullying
- Bridging the Generational Divide: Millennials vs. Boomers
- Ending Harassment and Retaliation in the Workplace

- Reality Based Decision Making for Effective Strategy Development
- How to De-escalate Conflicts Using Behavioral Science
- Why is Change so Hard?
- Principles of Humanistic Management
- 7 Sins of Staff Management
- How to Handle Cranky Customer Problems
- New Manager Orientation
- Humanist Group Leadership Lessons
- Sexual harassment training that works – general
- Sexual harassment training that works – AB 1825
- Stop Bullying in our Workplace – Staff Training
- Sexual Harassment Compliance Training
- No Fear Act training
- Planning for Personal Success!
- Talking to your child about death
- The Bully Vaccine Toolkit
- How to talk to your child's school about bullying
- Why Bullies Bully & How to Stop Them

CONNECT WITH ME ONLINE:
- Twitter: http://twitter.com/#!/JentheHumanist
- Facebook: http://www.facebook.com/JentheHumanist

- Or sign up for my mailing list:
  http://eepurl.com/c3LuI

The End

#####